To Brother Wesley Anderson,

So, You've Answered The Call??

Now What??

Blessings Alecceys
12.5-06
Rev ...

Rev. Andrew L. Foster, III., M. Div.

Note for Librarians: A cataloguing record for this book is available from Library and Archives Canada at www.collectionscanada.ca/amicus/index-e.html

ISBN 1-4120-7361-8

Printed in Victoria, BC, Canada. Printed on paper with minimum 30% recycled fibre. Trafford's print shop runs on "green energy" from solar, wind and other environmentally-friendly power sources.

TRAFFORD
PUBLISHING™

Offices in Canada, USA, Ireland and UK

This book was published *on-demand* in cooperation with Trafford Publishing. On-demand publishing is a unique process and service of making a book available for retail sale to the public taking advantage of on-demand manufacturing and Internet marketing. On-demand publishing includes promotions, retail sales, manufacturing, order fulfilment, accounting and collecting royalties on behalf of the author.

Book sales for North America and international:
Trafford Publishing, 6E–2333 Government St.,
Victoria, BC v8t 4p4 CANADA
phone 250 383 6864 (toll-free 1 888 232 4444)
fax 250 383 6804; email to orders@trafford.com
Book sales in Europe:
Trafford Publishing (uk) Limited, 9 Park End Street, 2nd Floor
Oxford, UK ox1 1hh UNITED KINGDOM
phone 44 (0)1865 722 113 (local rate 0845 230 9601)
facsimile 44 (0)1865 722 868; info.uk@trafford.com
Order online at:
trafford.com/05-2257

10 9 8 7 6 5 4 3

Rev. Andrew L. Foster, III.
So, You've Answered the Call??

Table of Contents

Dedication....................................1-5

Forward by First Lady Lorraine V. Foster................6-11

Introduction..................................12-14

My Calling...................................15-23

What's Your Style?..............................24-30

Delegate, Delegate, Delegate....................31-34

High Expectations..............................35-37

How to Say No Without Feeling Guilty.................38-40

Avoid Spiritual Bankruptcy.......................41-44

Overcoming Discouragement....................45-47

Danger, Danger, Danger.......................48-54

Burnout vs. Stress.............................55-58

Stress vs. Burnout.............................59-65

Rev. Andrew L. Foster, III.
So, You've Answered the Call??

Be Resilient..66-67

Recognizing Burnout......................................68-69

Time Management/Scheduling............................70-75

Vacations/Retreats..76-77

Guard Family Time...78-80

Physical Exercise...81-84

You Are What You Eat.....................................85-92

About the Author 93-98

Suggested Books to Read.................................99-101

Notes for Reflection & Application....................102-106

Blessings!!!

The Rev. Andrew L. Foster, III.

Dedication

"Withhold not good from them to whom it is

due, when it is in the power of

thine hand to do it."

Proverbs 3:27

Rev. Andrew L. Foster, III.
So, You've Answered the Call??

Dedication

I am greatly indebted to several persons who deserve to be named here. This book, my first endeavor at writing outside of a class syllabus, is dedicated to the memory of my grandfather and the patriarch of the Foster Family, Mr. Andrew L. Foster, Sr., who migrated North from the Eastern Shore of Maryland (Cambridge). Although he was not formally ordained, his was still a calling to serve God's people by word and deed.

This book is also dedicated in loving memory of my father, The Rev. Andrew L. Foster, Jr., (Blanche's child) who died on the battlefield of our Lord and Savior, Jesus Christ, while serving as the Senior Pastor of the First African Methodist Episcopal Zion (A.M.E.Z.) Church in Columbus, Ohio.

I also honor and lift up my best friend and partner in ministry, my wife, and my First Lady, Mrs. Lorraine Valencia Foster.

Lorraine has taught me the true meaning of Genesis 2:18; a help-meet, one that is suitable, and complementary.

Without her encouragement and support throughout our ministry serving the people of God; through pastoral visits, enduring my absence and long nights throughout three college degrees, this journey would have been a lonely endeavor at best. Who can find a virtuous woman, whose price is far above rubies? I know I have found such a jewel in Lorraine!

Finally, I dedicate this book to my Lord and Savior, whose blood was shed for my sins, and whose love, has given me an example to share the good news about salvation to the world and especially to my family.

Rev. Andrew L. Foster, III.
So, You've Answered the Call??

My prayer for all those that read this book, especially those that have yielded to the glorious privilege, of serving a Risen Savior is to discern the will of God for their lives, as it relates to ministry; understanding that God calls us to serve and to lead His people in a faithful and effective manner but not at the expense of our families.

"But if any provide not for his own, and especially for those of his own house, he hath denied the faith, and is worse than an infidel."

I Timothy 5:8

Rev. Andrew L. Foster, III.
So, You've Answered the Call??

Notes for Reflection & Application:

Rev. Andrew L. Foster, III.
So, You've Answered the Call??

*Forward By My Wife
And Best Friend,*

First Lady Lorraine Foster

Rev. Andrew L. Foster, III.
So, You've Answered the Call??

Forward

So You've Answered the Call Now What? After you have answered the call, what do you do? So many people that are entering ministry do not know what to do next. I pray that if you are that person, you will be assigned or connected to someone who has gone through the process; someone who knows the highs and lows of being in ministry, someone that will inspire you on how to better care for yourself while still doing effective ministry.

I pray that you are led to someone who will give you a copy of this book and say, "read this in your spare time, then let us discuss it when we next meet." Hopefully this is the book that will inspire you to go on and do greater things for the Lord, with better health and your family firmly beside you.

After my husband answered the call, the first thing he did was call his father.

He wanted to share the good news and to seek direction on where to go next. The response he received from his father was unexpected. His father said: "Son, I am happy for you as a father, but sad for you as a pastor." Of course my husband was stunned at the response.

Clearly this was not what he had expected to hear. My father-in-law then went on to explain that he was glad that my husband had come to realize that God is calling him and that he was happy that he finally answered the call on his life. The sadness that he alluded to was the reality that being a pastor can take a toll on your life and your family. Sadness because the burden of the congregation that he is to serve will be on him and sometimes it may seem difficult to bear; sadness because the church will take center stage and everything else will seem secondary.

Rev. Andrew L. Foster, III.
So, You've Answered the Call??

Two years later Reverend Andrew L. Foster, Jr. was called home to be with the Lord. He died of stress, heart disease, kidney failure and many other illnesses that could have been prevented if he had only taken time out to care for himself as he so diligently cared for God's people.

My husband, The Reverend Andrew L. Foster, III, came to a realization that God called him into ministry, but He did not call him at the expense of his health or his family. This is a message he wants all clergy to hear. To take care of themselves, take time out with their family. Read a good book, go to a movie, sit at your son's football or baseball game, watch your daughter in the school play, and take vacations away from the church yearly. This book is about eating properly, exercising, and maintaining a good healthy balance between family and church.

Rev. Andrew L. Foster, III.
So, You've Answered the Call??

I am so happy, and I feel truly blessed that God has placed this in him to learn all this early in his ministry. I have seen him evolve from a finicky eater to someone that is conscientious about what goes into his body, I have seen him struggle to exercise even though at times he is too tired to even think about it. I have seen him insist on taking two days off away from the church and keep his word by balancing family and ministry. I have seen him preparing for our family to go on vacation and instructing the leadership of the church not to call his cell phone because another pastor is on call in his absence.

Many seasoned pastors now say to him, how if only "they" had learned this early in their ministry, they would be better off now. Some have lost their spouses to illness and divorce. Some have strained relationships with their children; some are suffering from illnesses themselves, all because they did not take the time that is needed to care for themselves.

Rev. Andrew L. Foster, III.
So, You've Answered the Call??

My prayer for you is that as you read this book, you will find the importance of better clergy self care. I also pray that as you serve God's people, you will also serve yourself by maintaining your mind, body and soul.

His Faithful One,

First Lady Foster

Introduction

"That Christ may dwell in your hearts by faith; that ye, being rooted and grounded in love, May be able to comprehend with all saints what is the breadth, and length, and depth, and height; And to know the love of Christ, which passeth knowledge, that ye might be filled with all the fulness of God."

Ephesians 3:17-19

Rev. Andrew L. Foster, III.
So, You've Answered the Call??

Introduction

The title of this book, "So You've Answered The Call, Now What?" speaks first to me. I want nothing more than to serve God and His people; my passion is for Christ and the salvation of His people. I asked myself what are the steps or the process that will lead to a successful and faithful ministry; be it ordained ministry or lay ministry in the sight of our Lord, Jesus Christ?

What steps are necessary to ensure a healthy balance between family and ministry? What are the steps to be fully present with your family and fully present in the service of God?

The call to Christian Ministry, in my opinion, is the highest calling there is. It is more than a vocation and even at its best can be very challenging, rewarding and at the same time can be mentally, physically and spiritually draining.

Ministry can also be exhilarating and can also be lonely. It is full of joy and at times it can bring rivers of tears that no box of tissues can dry up. Ministry in itself is a paradox. The simple act of service can bring you to a place of needing to be served.

It is my hope and fervent prayer that this book will serve you the reader as another tool you can place in your ministry tool box, to bring you closer to the awesome privilege and high honor of serving God with your whole heart, mind, body and soul.

"The Lord bless thee, and keep thee: The Lord make his face shine upon thee, and be gracious unto thee: The Lord lift up his countenance upon thee, and give thee peace." Numbers 6:24-26

Blessings Always!!!

The Rev. Andrew L. Foster, III., M.Div.
Ordained Elder in the United Methodist Church

My Calling

"Before I formed thee in the belly I knew
thee; and before thou camest forth out of the
womb I sanctified thee, and I ordained thee a
prophet unto the nations."

Jeremiah 1:5

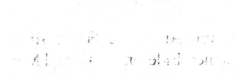

My Calling

I like many of you that are reading this book, are Preacher's or Pastor's Kids (PK's); and if not, have an active role in the church. I did not have the luxury of choosing whether or not to attend church or bible study. In fact when the doors of the church were open, my family was there, sometimes for the entire day. I have always had a love for the church, for God and His people, but never dreamed of or considered being a Pastor.

My call to Ordained Ministry began in my mother's womb according to Jeremiah 1:5 - "Before I formed thee in the belly I knew thee; and before thou camest forth out of the womb I sanctified thee, and I ordained thee a prophet unto the nations." It took thirty-five years of wrestling with the Spirit of the Living God, to acknowledge what was already present in my life.

Rev. Andrew L. Foster, III.
So, You've Answered the Call??

I am the son of a preacher, the sixth generation of Methodist preachers and I saw the church from both sides and did not have a desire to be a part of the "system."

As I grew in the knowledge of Jesus Christ through bible study, prayer and soul searching, I could no longer run from what was my purpose and designed plan in life, to be a minister of the gospel.

My theology is framed more or less, but not limited to the following two passages of Scripture, 2 Timothy 2:15: which compels me to study to show myself approved unto God, a workman not ashamed of the gospel, rightly dividing the word of truth. These instructions given to young Timothy have allowed me to see that I too, must be in a study mode, an attitude of absorbing all the tools necessary to be an effective witness for my Lord and Savior.

In my daily Christian journey, I continue to realize that the more I study, the more I find out just how much I don't know.

The second passage of scripture that helps me to define my theology is Proverbs 3:27, which tells me not to withhold good from them that deserve it, when it is in my power to help them.

This reminds me that all of God's people are of value and deserve good and are guaranteed through the Spirit of God, to have their spiritual and physical needs met. It also confirms that God and the Holy Spirit are no respecter of persons - what He has done for one, He will surely do for another.

My call to ministry has been confirmed to me through the Holy Spirit, that I am to be a vehicle, a tool, a conduit providing some sense and type of solace and peace to God's people through the teaching and preaching of the Gospel.

My call to ministry is furthered enhanced as I am afforded the privilege of serving God's people in the pulpit, the hospitals, the nursing homes, the private homes, and in whatever setting I am placed. Like Jabez in I Chronicles 4:10, my territory is truly expanding and enlarging, because God has blessed me indeed, His hands have kept me from evil. I see my calling as a J-O-Y and not as a J-O-B!

I accepted the Lord as my personal Savior at the age of 21 while serving in the United States Air Force. Looking back over my life, I realize that I was not as faithful to God as I should have been when I first accepted Him as my Lord and personal Savior. I did not keep the promises I made when I was baptized. Thankfully, God through His abundant grace and mercy forgave my sins of commission as well as omission. He knew what the future held for me, in spite of my disobedience. (Jeremiah 29:11)

Rev. Andrew L. Foster, III.
So, You've Answered the Call??

I come from a long line of Methodist preachers and now realize in a real way, that the fruit truly does not fall far from the tree. (Train up a child in the way he should go: and when he is old, he will not depart from it - Proverbs 22:6). I was always told at an early age that I would be a preacher, but I like most preachers today, responded "Not Me!" I have always had the will to serve God and His people, but not in a formal way.

When I left the military in 1985, I renewed my membership status at the church where I was baptized as a child. I immediately become an active participant by joining the Senior Usher Board and later became a Sunday School teacher. During my journey, I have held various leadership positions in the church including: Evangelism chair, Interim Church School Superintendent, Director of Vacation Bible School, Class Leader, Boy Scout Leader, First Vice President of the Senior Usher Board, Youth Coordinator and member of the Adult Gospel Chorus.

Rev. Andrew L. Foster, III.
So, You've Answered the Call??

I believe these past and present experiences have furthered my convictions to pursue a theological education. As an African American male, it was always impressed in my mind to work harder and to strive for excellence in every area of my life.

This work ethic was modeled by my godly grandparents (Mom-Mom and Pop-Pop) as well as my mother, Patricia and father, Andrew. As I moved through my adolescence years, the tendency to value and appreciate hard work was reinforced every day. My father often shared this philosophy with me: When able, work smarter and not harder. Utilize the skills, the tools and the gifts God has given you and you will be able to work smarter.

I have come to appreciate this wisdom greatly. I am no stranger to working hard, however, working smarter tends to increase your life span.

Rev. Andrew L. Foster, III.
So, You've Answered the Call??

When I became a Christian, my work ethic and all the lessons learned were transferred into my work for God. I had a desire to do all that I could to honor and please God.

My acceptance and acknowledgment of the call to Christian Ministry was revealed to me on Sunday, August 10, 1997 (Yes, I remember the date), at Tindley Temple United Methodist Church (founded by the late Reverend Dr. Charles Albert Tindley; renowned preacher and hymnwriter) during a sermon delivered by my pastor, The Rev. Dr. Claude A. Edmonds, now a retired Elder in the United Methodist Church. I had heard the very same sermon many times before, but I had never received it in the way I did on that day. I realized that God was instructing me by confirmation through the message that I had to stop running, stop making excuses and enter the Ministry by faith and by trusting in Him that He would order my steps and even direct my path.

What Mark Are You Leaving?

By Bill Hybels

If you're a dad, what kind of mark are you leaving on your children, especially your sons? Do you realize that your little boys are watching you like hawks? They're trying to figure out what maleness is all about, and you're their model. I hope they see in you a deep, uncompromising love for God. I hope they see both toughness and tenderness, If they do, then you have served them well. Your little girls, too will benefit because they'll grow up with a clear vision of the kind of men who make godly husbands.

Notes for Reflection & Application:

Rev. Andrew L. Foster, III.
So, You've Answered the Call??

What's Your Style?

"In matters of style,
swim with the current;
in matters of principle,
stand like a rock."

Thomas Jefferson

What's Your Style?

Understanding who you are as well as your mission statement is crucial to your ministry. Equally as important is understanding who you are as a leader, and fine tuning your leadership style.

Who you are as a leader is greatly impacted by lots of external forces. People you encounter in ministry help to define your leadership style. Certainly God has given us spiritual gifts to help discern who we are as leaders. As with any process towards a desired outcome, there are different steps or levels of leadership.

All of us have been through what is called an Introductory of Beginning Leadership stage. This is a time of gathering the necessary tools to be utilized later in ministry. The beginning leader might be young, or an older, second career person.

Even while the beginning leader is gaining new insight, ministry should still be taking place.

Another level or stage in leadership is the Assimilating Leader. This stage of leadership is where the leader continues to acquire leadership tools and further develops or enhances those tools already practiced. Just as a soldier needs an array of tools and equipment; to be effective in ministry, a good leader should choose the right "weapons" for spiritual warfare.

Another area of leadership is the Building Leader. The building leader is at that point in their ministry when more emphasis and focus is on doing ministry rather than preparing for ministry. It is often recommended that we revisit both the beginning and assimilating stages to review where we have been, in order to be discern where we need to go.

In the United Methodist Church, each time you receive a new appointment to a new parish, you are actually in a sense once again a beginner. The building leader takes those tools that have been acquired and mastered and begins to build something with them.

Still another stage of leadership is the Achieving Leader. This stage of leadership is a step beyond merely building something with leadership tools. In this step, the leader is doing that which God has called them and equipped them to do when they were in their mother's womb (Jeremiah 1:5). I must caution you at this stage; achievement is not measured by the size of your church building or how many people you have on the membership roles, nor is it measured by the length of time served in ministry. Becoming an achieving leader means the leader is doing what God has prepared them to do. True success in ministry is discovered in your faithfulness to the One that called you in the first place.

Another stage of leadership is called the Maturing Leader. In this level of leadership, it is more than just surviving to maturity in years of service. It should be a time when the leader has gathered enough tools for their arsenal and practiced experience, to consider becoming a Paul for the up and coming Timothy's of the world. In this level of leadership, it is a time of sharing, reflecting and should also be a time of celebrating all that God has done in and through their lives. The maturing leader may be entering some of the most productive years in kingdom building.

Lastly, the Focusing Leader. This type of leader is not ready to stop serving God as a kingdom leader. Instead, they are ready for a new focus or a new direction in ministry. This pastor may or not want to continue active service within a local church. Many faithful pastors have served in a capacity outside the local church, and I might add with excellence.

Some focusing leaders have moved from the local mission fields to service in other countries.

The question that only you can answer is: Where are you on the leadership path? Understanding your leadership style will greatly enhance your ministry experience and will truly be a blessing to those you are called to serve. Rather than attempting to be something that you are not, you would do well to think of leadership styles as tools to be used when appropriate.

Every pastor, if they wish to be effective must learn different styles of leadership. A good leader will be able to direct, coach, support and delegate. My favorite of course is delegating. As a delegating leader, you actually give so much authority to team members that you trust them to make decisions and solve problems without your direct involvement.

Rev. Andrew L. Foster, III.
So, You've Answered the Call??

As a pastor, pray that you are blessed with faithful volunteers or a paid staff who can function well under delegating leadership.

Whatever leadership you choose or grow into, approach it with humility and seek the guidance of the Holy Spirit.

Notes for Reflection & Application:

Delegate, Delegate, Delegate

"Do all the good you can, by all
the means you can, in all the ways
you can, in all the places you can, to
all the people you can, as long as you can"

John Wesley

Delegate, Delegate, Delegate

Some church members expect their pastors to be superhuman; able to leap tall buildings with a single prayer; faster than a stewardship locomotive. As a Minister of the Gospel, the resident theologian, you are expected to be preacher, teacher, leader, business manager, caring pastor, active community member, referee and much more. Of course, the standard is often too high.

One of the best pieces of advice I can share that was given to me, is to realize that I can't do everything; and I'm only a part of God's plan, not God's whole plan.

A wise pastor can grow their ministry by involving others in working toward the mission of the church. In many churches, the pastor leads a staff team. It only makes sense to delegate or distribute some of the responsibilities to the church staff.

I must caution you before you begin to assign different tasks to your staff. First you must be sure that the staff fully understands the mission of the church you are serving. Next, there must be a great commitment to one another in relationship of trust. Finally, there should be an intentional element of spiritual growth through discussion and spiritual retreats.

Delegating to staff members should be based on their job description and not those things you don't feel like doing. If the delegation is based upon their job description, then the staff member will have a sense of confidence in their area of responsibility.

Reporting and evaluation must also be practiced when delegating; remember you can delegate authority to do a particular assignment, but the ultimate responsibility is yours as the senior pastor.

Delegating can be difficult if you are not willing to let go. In a small but growing church, the pastor has always led the Adult Sunday School, taught the Adult Bible Study Classes, Facilitated the new members' training classes, led the evangelism efforts in the community, attending the meetings outside the church to be a presence in the community, etc. As the church grows, the need for a minister of education or a youth pastor becomes evident.

If you remember to delegate, you will be far better at regulating the scale of harmony needed to maintain a healthy balance in your ministry.

Notes for Reflection & Application:

High Expectations

"I press toward the mark for the prize of the high calling of God in Christ Jesus."
Philip. 3:14

High Expectations

Jesus reminds us in the Gospel of St. Luke 12:48b, For everyone to whom much is given, from him much will be required; and to whom much has been committed, of him they will ask the more." Christian ministry has always been a frighten away vocation, in which who you are matters more than what you know or what skills you may have.

The Pastoral Epistles give us great examples as Timothy receives instructions from Paul to "set an example in speech and conduct, in love, in faith, in purity" (1 Timothy 4:12). Applied to this present day, in an age of mis-speak, gross speak, down speak, and outright lying, be a model in what you say. Speak the truth in love (Ephesians 4:15). Let your word be "Yes, Yes, or No, No (Matthew 5:37).

As my grandfather used to tell me, let your word be your bond; even if you are broke, your word is worth more than silver and gold! Silver and gold, you may not have, but your word, you surely can keep.

As minsters of the gospel, you must be above reproach, honorable in all our relations. In an age where covenants are broken almost as quickly as they are made, stand by your commitments. Do not be blown away by every wind; be steadfast and unmovable in your convictions and your calling.

Notes for Reflection & Application:

Rev. Andrew L. Foster, III.
So, You've Answered the Call??

How to Say No,
Without Feeling Guilty

"If anyone considers himself religious
and yet does not keep a tight reign of his tongue,
he deceives himself and his religion is
worthless."

James 1:26

Rev. Andrew L. Foster, III.
So, You've Answered the Call??

How to Say No, Without Feeling Guilty

There will be times in your ministry when you will be bombarded with all kinds of requests; requests from your parishioners, requests from your colleagues, requests from people you don't even know and of course requests from your family.

I have learned that is better to say, let me get back to you, instead of agreeing to accommodate at a moments notice. When you must deny a request, it does not mean that you are a bad person; it simply means you are aware of your limitations, and that is a good thing. It is far better for you to deny a request, especially when it is not in your ability to fulfill the petition.

I would challenge you to think in terms of what is the best outcome; how will saying yes to this request have a lasting impact on my health, my family, and of course my ministry.

Rev. Andrew L. Foster, III.
So, You've Answered the Call??

There should be no room for guilt if a request must be denied. Knowing that God knows your heart, should alleviate you from the unnecessary feelings of guilt associated with "letting someone down."

Notes for Reflection & Application:

Avoid Spiritual Bankruptcy

"And he said unto them, Come ye yourselves
apart into a desert place, and rest a while: for
there were many coming and going, and they
had no leisure so much as to eat."

Mark 6:31

Avoid Spiritual Bankruptcy

Bankruptcy is a case where bills and debt greatly exceed your ability to pay. It is being so far behind with absolutely no way of catching up. It can be called financial failure, insolvency, defaulting, economic death or financial disaster. As a minister of the Gospel, you can find yourself in a state of spiritual bankruptcy. It happens, more often than reported.

You need a plan to avoid spiritual bankruptcy. Here are a few suggestions. You must engage in daily personal devotion (this is not the same as preparing for preaching or teaching). Quality and quantity time with God will make your spirit ready for the battles of the day (I know the battle is not yours, but you should still be prepared). Personal devotions is a regular time of listening to God through Scripture and prayer. If this is done, you will develop a spiritual reserve and find the resources to minister because of your personal time with God.

Your personal time with God will help you maintain perspective in all the busy demands of your ministry. Personal devotions are a great stress buffer. Along with personal devotions, you will also need plenty of rest. I know rest is a four letter word, but you must have both physical and emotional rest to avoid spiritual bankruptcy.

Physically to be your spiritual best, you must have adequate rest. Power naps or cat naps will not suffice. Sleep allows your body time to rebuild and refresh. Research indicates about seven and one half hours of sleep is optimal to maintain your physical integrity.

The other type of rest is time away. Mark 6:31 tells of Jesus' word of advice to come away for a time of rest. Make time to get away, find a quiet place for leisure. Move away from a schedule of sick calls, funerals, sermon preparation, counseling, putting out spiritual fires, and committee meetings.

You may be blessed to find two or three hours a week just to listen to God, to reflect and to anticipate the days ahead.

Remember that a minister, who is constantly around others, cannot effectively continue to minister to others.

Lastly, develop strong accountability relationships with people that encourage and nurture you. You may choose to be accountable in such ways as devoting time to your spouse, time with your children, personal devotion, or exercise. Your spiritual well-being impacts your social, mental and physical well-being. When you are at your best spiritually, you feel better physically and mentally, and you are able to relate better to others when your spiritual bank account has a surplus and not a deficit.

Notes for Reflection & Application:

Overcoming Discouragement

"And let us not be weary in well doing: for in due season we shall reap, if we faint not."

Galatians 6:9

Overcoming Discouragement

The Apostle Paul said in Galatians 6:9; "Let us not grow weary in well doing for in due season we shall reap, if we faint not." The law of the harvest says if we keep planting good seed in good soil, in God's time there will be fruit.

As clergy, we must understand that not all fields are equally productive. You may be serving in what seems to be a difficult place. The people around you may be hardened and calloused. Nevertheless, we are called to work no matter where we are, no mater how great or little the harvest may be. Our task as ministers of the gospel is to be faithful to God, to plant good seed in the soil around us, and to let God handle the amount and the quality of the harvest. I would caution you not to measure success in ministry by comparing yourself to other pastors and other churches. To do so, would only create a sense of pride if you do better than they or jealousy, envy and despair if you do worse.

Success in the kingdom of God is measured by faithfulness, and not by how many names are on the role. If your goal is to please God and not man, than you will never be discouraged in your ministry. Remember the work you do as a pastor is kingdom work; God's kingdom, and not your own. Depend on God for the strength to overcome discouragement.

In 1 John 5:4, John said, "This is the victory that overcomes the world, even our faith." Discouragement is a powerful tool of Satan, the Devil, the Evil One. He uses it to immobilize God's pastors, but God is still God, and we are still His servants, so remember you are more than a conqueror!!

Notes for Reflection & Application:

Rev. Andrew L. Foster, III.
So, You've Answered the Call??

Danger!! Danger!! Danger!!

"Watch ye therefore, and pray always, that ye
may be accounted worthy to escape all these
things that shall come to pass,
and to stand before the Son of man."
Matthew 26:41

Danger!! Danger!! Danger!!

In the mid 70's, there was a television sitcom called, "Lost in Space". In this sitcom, the family robot was always seemed to be present to point out potential signs of intrusion or possible signs of danger to the Robinson family. Unfortunately, the clergy person has no such mechanical device to warn of potential dangers to our person or to our families. We do, however, have the Holy Spirit, and a wealth of Stress Self-Assessment Tools, that can greatly enhance our ability to maintain a healthy balance between Family and Ministry. (Notice I said, Family First)

Christian Leadership can be filled with great stress. Roy Oswald has put his finger on stress experienced by pastors as he writes:

> Pastors are in a people-related profession in which our value to others is our ability to get down in

the trenches with them when the bombs are dropping all around. In addition to being there for people through all the joys and traumas of their lives, we are expected somehow, by magic, to keep everybody happy and make our congregations grow. All of this in a post-Christian/Jewish culture that no longer holds in high esteem men and women of the cloth. If we are not stressed to a greater or lesser degree, we aren't in touch with reality.[1]

There are all types of stress, and no matter where they originate, they have the potential of triggering, and causing an imbalance in your system. Someone once said that grace and mercy will follow you all the days of your life,

---

[1] Roy M. Oswald, Clergy Self-Care: Finding a Balance for Effective Ministry (New York: Alban Institute, 1991), 26.

and as a pastor, another twin will follow you as well: stress and burnout, if you are not able to discern when to be still, and know that God is God!

When something unsettling or unnerving happens in our environment, in our world, in our space, the hypothalamus of our brain triggers the automatic nervous system, and the endocrine-gland system, which then prepares our bodies to either stand our ground and fight, or take the high road and run. All types of stress, no matter what their sources begin a kind of domino effect on our bodies. We must listen to the danger signs.

Commonly, when we experience stress, our blood pressure elevates, our heart begins to beat rapidly, our liver begins to dump sugar and cholesterol into our bloodstream for added energy; our pupils begin to dilate and our stomachs stop digesting.

If we are ever to maintain a healthy balance between family and ministry, we must become aware of the specific ways stress affects us. We not only need to pinpoint the specific stressors in our day to day ministry; we will also need to find the self-care strategies that will work to reduce, and if possible eliminate our stress. If we are successful in managing our stress, it will not only lengthen your life, it will increase the quality of your life as well. A body that is intentional on being aware of the things that cause unnecessary and unwanted stress, will be a body that looks better physically, a body that will have better weight and muscle tone. It will be a body that participates in eating the right foods and exercising will become second nature. I am not saying that this will be an easy task, however, I am saying that you will feel better, live longer and be more effective in ministry, and more importantly your family and loved ones will have the joy of your presence much longer than if you chose not to listen to the danger signs.

Effective stress management will not only lengthen your life span, it will increase the quality of your life. Managing the stress in your life will not be an easy assignment. It will require dedication and commitment. The driving force, the motivation behind all the work must be a determination to gain control of your life and live it in a more holistic, and healthy fashion. Those around you, your family, your co-workers, and your congregation will undoubtedly benefit in the long run.

Stress is an equal opportunity dis-abler. It does not discriminate or exclude anyone. When you have bypassed your threshold of stress, you are a disaster waiting to happen, a walking time bomb. It is not merely fate, that someone has a heart attack or some other illness. More often than not, disease strikes an unhealthy body than a healthy one. So, how do we know when we have crossed the line, bypassed our threshold of stress? First, we must know ourselves.

We must be in touch with our body and listen to the warning signs and take heed. One way that has been helpful to me in knowing myself is by keeping a journal. Recording the times in my life when I felt unhealthy, overly tired and drained, kept me aware of the condition of my body.

If you really think about it, when we go to the doctor's office, the first thing they do after taking your temperature and blood pressure is ask you how you feel? Have you been experiencing any unusual pains or discomfort? By tracking our own health, we in essence become our best gauge in determining our physical makeup.

Notes for Reflection & Application:

Burnout vs. Stress

Burnout vs. Stress

There is a difference between burnout and stress. Stress and burnout deplete your body, your mind and your soul. Stress taxes our adjustment abilities and burnout taxes our ability to continue caring. Burnout is the result of chronic or habitual stress. No matter how much you may think you are in control of your faculties, if a person remains in a stressful situation for an extended period, burnout is sure to follow. Burnout decreases your energy, your self-esteem, and causes you to be cynical, skeptical and very negative.

It is documented that burnout tends to be the disease of choice for the helping professions: social workers, teachers, nurses, police workers, court appointed lawyers, therapists, physicians, and yes clergy!

The key factor or similarity of these professions as it relates to burnout seems to be control. Does the person in those aforementioned vocations have control over how many needy and hurting people they come in contact with? Most of the time, the answer is No!

Typically, as clergy, we begin our ministries with hope and a lot of high energy. In our enthusiasm, we often forget to take care of ourselves. After all, the Psalmist did say, that the zeal of the Lord consumes me.

As pastors, we must realize that ministry is conducted within the confines and the limits of our human bodies. Having bodies that are not immortal, means that we will be vulnerable to sickness, fatigue, disease, and even death. The difference between a committed an over-committed person is that the over-committed person will not listen to the physical signs of being stretched to the limit.

As clergy and believers in Jesus Christ, we have the best example to emulate. Jesus knew when he needed to withdraw and be in a quiet place, whether it was a garden, asleep on a boat, or a mountain top, Jesus knew how to keep balance in his ministry, and so should we.

Burnout is nothing to be ashamed of. Every effective and committed religious leader has experienced one form of burnout out or another. Moses experienced burnout, Saul, the King of Israel experienced burnout and the prophet Jeremiah was no different.

So how do you reverse or prevent burnout? One way is to know your limitations. Accept who you are, know what you can and cannot do. Seasoned clergy have told me that know one ever told them about burnout. Seminaries didn't teach it, and congregations don't want to understand it.

Rev. Andrew L. Foster, III.
So, You've Answered the Call??

You can reverse the trend of burnout in your ministry if you avail yourself of any and all clergy self care material. Even if you learn only one way, to prevent or reverse burnout, it will be worth it in the end; just ask your family!

Notes for Reflection & Application:

Stress vs. Burnout

Stress vs. Burnout

Stress on the other hand, occurs when too much change or freshness forces people to overestimate their adjustment capacities and after awhile, they become either physically or emotionally ill. Stress for the person in ministry is not reserved only for the clergy person, it has a way of creeping and finding its way into the family.

The following refers to Clergy. Role Ambiguity: when pastors have an unclear picture of their role they work harder to cover all the bases; Role Conflict: pastoral expectations often conflict with personal or family expectations; Role Overload: pastors become overwhelmed by all the expectations of parishioners; Time Demands: clergy are on call twenty-four hours a day, seven days a week, making planning difficult; Lack of Pastoral Care:

most clergy do not have a good mentor or solid spiritual advisor; Lack of Opportunities for Extra Dependence: clergy need opportunities to de-role and be taken care of; Geographical Relocation: when you move, almost everything changes, requiring sometimes massive adjustments; Political/Economic Uncertainty: much of your future depends on your relationship with a particular parish; A Helping Profession: those in the helping professions burn out more often than other professionals: Loneliness: beyond fellow clergy, very few persons understand the role of parish pastor or the demands of pastoral work. The aforementioned stressors are only the tip of the ice burg.

The clergy spouse equally, have their share of stressors. Role Expectation: parishioners have certain ideas about how the minister's spouse should behave;

Surrogate Clergy: when the ordained person is
unavailable, lay persons sometimes unload their
anxiety on the available spouse; Super Person:
the person married to the minister often manages
several roles including manager of the home-
front and other roles within the church;
Geographical Relocation: clergy spouses are
often affected more negatively by a move than
clergy. Clergy have a more clearly defined role
and get involved immediately; its more for
difficult for a spouse to find their way; Lack of
Support: support for the spouse in the parish
may be inadequate at best; Parsonage Living:
when your home belongs to the parish; how you
use the home may be scrutinized; Finances:
because of low pastor salaries, many spouses are
forced to seek employment even when they have
small children at home.

One of the great givers of stress can be
ourselves. The way we deal with what is
important to us can create anxiety. Often stress
can build up in a kind of subconscious way. It
sneaks up on you.

You begin to notice uneasiness building. Things just don't seem to be going right. The stress builds, and you are not sure why. Or it may be blatant and meet you head on.

Stress can be traced to the difference between what you believe is important and what requires most of your energy. If we fail to manage our stress, the stress will manage us. When we consistently exceed our stress thresholds, we lose our capacity to function at optimum levels. Some of the effects are: decrease in perception; perceived loss of options; regression in infantile behavior; inability to make changes in destructive relationship patterns; fatigue, depression, and physical illness.

Stress can be handled in several ways. The Bible says, "As a man thinketh, so is he." Perception can be the filter for all your decisions, attitudes, and actions.

Reality and perception are not the same. A gap exists between what is real and what you perceive. Check the reality of your perception. The next time you face a stressful situation, answer the following questions. As you answer them, consider yourself, your family, and your ministry in the short and long term.

What is the immediate value or consequence of the situation? What will be the consequences of the same situation tomorrow? What will be the value of a decision next week? What will be the value in one year? What will be the value five years from now?

Another method to manage stress is by being pro-active. People with this trait don't wait for bad things to occur, they try to correct them before they happen. Pro-active people will anticipate change and plan for ways to take advantage of that change, as opposed to feeling unable to do anything, which leads to a feeling of helplessness.

Stress can also be managed by seeing possibilities instead of pitfalls. This is not a quick fix. It is a way of thinking, approaching and viewing all that comes your way in ministry, both your agenda and God's agenda. This way of thinking is fueled by gaining a sense of growth, mastery and accomplishment from solving the "puzzles" that are always present.

Conversely, seeing life's problems as threats holds back the work of the kingdom. If you are afraid, something is not going to work, that an idea will not be accepted, or that program or ministry might not be exactly perfect, you'll never get anywhere. Threat is the trick of the devil. It will paralyze you from moving in the direction God has ordered you take. The Psalmist said, "I will instruct you and teach you in the way which you should go." and the prophet Jeremiah, reminds you that "I know the plans that I have for you, says the Lord, plans for welfare not for calamity, to give you a future and a hope."

Rev. Andrew L. Foster, III.
So, You've Answered the Call??

One of the joys of ministry is finding your purpose as it relates to the will of God. Throughout Scripture God has given Ministers of the Gospel all the resources needed to be effective in ministry, for truly God equips those that He calls to His service. I am convinced that ministry can not be done alone; even the Lone Ranger had his Tonto.

If God has blessed you with a spouse, children, an extended family; then I would submit that God intended for you to be in a balanced relationship, as it relates to family and ministry. Quite simply, I believe God wants us to be good stewards of that which He has entrusted unto us!

Notes for Reflection & Application:

Be Resilient

Be Resilient

Resilience is the strong ability to cope and adapt during times of depravation, adversity and of course stress. Resilience is the ability to get through the high stress periods of changed and come out on the other side with a greater sense of well-being.

Someone once said, there's a blessing in your pressing! In other words, as a pastor, it would do you a great deal of good if you learn how to be resilient.

A person who is able to press on and do God's will, doing what's right in God's eyes, without fear or reluctance to rely on others is a person that can handle stress. There is a definite need to develop a network of friends, including one or more confidants.

A few good friends can mean a world of difference in your stress level. Simply knowing that they are there if the need should arise to talk and more importantly to listen, may be all the support you need.

Another strategy for managing your stress, is to commit yourself to reading the Bible everyday (I don't mean reading the Bible in order to prepare for your sermons). Read the Psalms, Read Romans, read and reread the Scriptures for encouragement, especially Psalm 37, and Jeremiah 29, with emphasis on verse 11.

Notes for Reflection & Application:

Recognizing Burnout

Recognizing Burnout

Burnout is when you are completely empty. You are spiritually, emotionally and physically poured out. There is nothing left to offer. As pastors, you will experience some form of burnout in your ministry. It is important to recognize some ways you can become burned out.

The following is a list of ten danger signs: your devotional life is suffering; your family life is being adversely affected; you have a nagging sense of ever being behind; you find yourself with a low threshold for inconvenience, Sabbath rest is the exception and not the norm; you experience a sense of overall weariness; physical exercise is sporadic or nonexistent; physical ailments are increasing; the sense of serving God with Joy is gone; you fight periodic thoughts of fleeing from the will of God.

Recognizing these signs of burnout is one thing, dealing with them is quite another.

The following list will aid you in avoiding the aforementioned list. Wait on God as a necessity, not a nicety; see the home as the launching pad for all public ministry; recognize the need for supportive relationships; remember that character must precede charisma, commit yourself to build for permanence; learn to plan, delegate, and manage your time; plan time off carefully and creatively; be released to say no, make exercise and proper nutrition and integral part of your life; and stay in your sphere of expertise and resist the snare of comparison.

Notes for Reflection & Application:

Time Management/Scheduling

"Six days shalt thou labour, and do all thy work: But the seventh day is the sabbath of the Lord thy God: in it thou shalt not do any work, thou, nor thy son, nor thy daughter, thy manservant, nor thy maidservant, nor thy cattle, nor thy stranger that is within thy gates:"

Exodus 20:9-10

Time Management/Scheduling

I Corinthians 14:40 reminds us to "let everything be done decently and in order." I would suggest that also applies to the scheduling of your day.

Time managed means time saved; that means more time for pastoral ministry, growth, study, and of course family. As a pastor, you will receive many invitations to attend many functions; invitations from your congregation, invitations from your fellow clerics, invitations from your community and civic leaders. Your appointment calendar, your palm pilot, pocket pc, or even a protective secretary can be a very useful tool in providing some needed relief during a busy day at the office.

If someone approaches you, particularly at the last minute, to attend an event or perform a task that is clearly outside your ability to accommodate, don't be so quick to respond in the affirmative (as pastor's that is usually our initial response), give yourself time to check with your means of scheduling. Another helpful tip in managing your calendar is to block out time for personal devotion, prayer, pleasure reading (outside of the Bible), and for silence and solitude, which produces more creative work and creative results.

If these essential elements are built into your normal work week, you will find more than enough time for everything else. Scripture affirms this as evident in Psalm 46:10, which says, "Be still and know that I am God; and in addition to the Psalmist, Isaiah (30:15) reminds us of the following: "In returning and rest you shall be saved, in quietness and in trust shall be your strength."

The metaphors that Jesus used in his three years of active ministry are frequently images of the single, the small, and the quiet, which have effects far greater in their appearance: salt, leaven, and seeds. Unfortunately, our culture (western) promotes the opposite emphasis: the big, the grandiose, and the noisy.

As pastors, it is an absolute necessity, that we deliberately ally ourselves with the quiet, and not leap head-first into every invitation extended to us. There is a greater need to develop the skills contained in Holy Scripture and learn the quietness and the attentiveness that comes by being in the constant presence of God.

Assign priorities. Ecc. 3:1 tells us "to everything there is a ...time", but not all matters and events under the heavens have equal importance or worth. Assigning priorities help guide how valuable time should be spent. Since we do not know what tomorrow will bring, we must also learn not to procrastinate.

Avoid putting off working on high priority issues. Procrastination behaviors can include day dreaming or making a "to do list" (not the same as planning).

Procrastination is often a product of dread, fear, fatigue, lack of interest, or a quest for perfection. Get in the habit of planning your work and then working your plan. Time management can make a world of difference in your ministry. The greatest reminder for time management is found in Psalm 90:12; "So teach us to number our days."

Alex MacKenzie, in a ten year study of time utilization found a significant relationship between how managers use their time and their levels of stress. He identified seven danger signals of stress, and indicates that if we experience three or four of these, our stress level is probably high, and poor time management may be the cause:

1. The belief that we are indispensable.

2. No time for important tasks. Crisis consistently robs us of time for top priorities.

3. Attempting too much. We constantly underestimate the time needed and effort it will take to complete tasks. An inability to say, "No" is part of this. We think we can do it all.

4. Constant unrelenting pressure. We always feel we're behind and won't be able to get on top of our job.

5. Habitual long hours.

6. Guilt about leaving work early.

7. Taking worry home with us. We are physically at home, but our minds are back on the job. Preoccupying worries of the day take precedence over family and personal activities.[2]

---

[2] R. Alex MacKenzie, MacKenzie on Time (cassette) "How to Save Two Hours a Day, " (Allentown, PA 18001, Day Timers, 1979).

Vacation/Retreats

<u>Vacation/Retreats</u>

If you want to remain focused and energized to do ministry, then you must take your vacations. A vacation does not include toting your appointment book, palm pilot, lap top or other means of scheduling meetings. You actually do a disservice to your congregation and your family if you are focused on ministry 24/7. I know what you are thinking: "I don't have time to take a vacation."

I challenge you to see things from a different vantage point and ask yourself, if you have the time to wait in the doctor's office for your results of an operation that could have been avoided if only you took a vacation to download from the everyday stressors of ministry. Ask yourself, if you have the time to rebuild your marriage, your family and give back the "memory" moments your children need to grow.

Ask yourself, if God would have it this way. Maybe you are thinking that taking a vacation is too costly. I have learned that a vacation does not always mean traveling abroad, or taking a cruise. A vacation can simply be driving upstate or down south. A vacation can simply be riding bicycles with your family, eating water ice on a park bench, catching a movie or simply doing something you've always wanted to do.

The English call a vacation a holiday; why not take advantage of as many holidays as you can to strengthen your family ties, because remember when the church is not there, your family will be.

Notes for Reflection & Application:

Rev. Andrew L. Foster, III.
So, You've Answered the Call??

Guard Family Time

Albert Einstein said,
"There are two ways to live life.
One is as though nothing is a miracle.
The other is as though everything is a miracle."

Everything that God has given
to you is a miracle. Cherish the miracle
of family...

Guard Family Time

Keeping the boundaries between family and ministry is a tall task for clergy. This is more difficult especially if you live in the church parsonage or even in the same community. One boundary that is crucial to your balance is to establish and protect your quality and quantity family time outside of the church.

As a clergy person, you must regard your family time as more important than your church appointments. This can be challenging because some parishioners may not value the pastor's family time as a high priority in comparison to the many demands on the pastor.

If you are to maintain a healthy balance between family and ministry you must be intentional in planning for quality family times and mark them in bold and red letters on your calendars.

When scheduling conflicts occur, and they will, do not get in the habit of apologizing for keeping your commitment made to your family.

Another area to be aware of is your families' privacy. Avoid using family illustrations in the public arena. Advise church members to use your home phone number for emergencies only (be sure to define clearly what an emergency is; stubbing your toe at 2 A.M. and calling the pastor for prayer is not an emergency).

Remember, your family will be there when your congregation is no where to be found.

Notes for Reflection & Application:

Physical Exercise

<u>Physical Exercise</u>

Someone has said that the lack of physical exercise is considered by doctors to be the most serious health hazard among North Americans. This includes clergy too! In 1989, the Center for Disease Control in Atlanta reported that at least five of the eleven physical fitness goals set in the 80s would not be met by the 90s (remember that new year's resolution).

It is has been documented that regular physical exercise reduces the incidence of many medical conditions, and almost notably aids in fighting heart disease, colon cancer, diabetes, and obesity.

According to aerobic specialist, and trainers, we need at least twenty minutes of exercise three times a week to keep our cardiovascular systems healthy.

During these exercise periods we need to increase our heart rate to about 120 beats per minute. We need additional exercise to keep our weight in check or develop muscle tone, but those sessions of heavy breathing are the minimum for cardiovascular fitness.

When we fail to exercise vigorously three or four times a week our hearts become weak and have to work much harder to get the blood through our system. With proper exercise, our hearts become stronger, so that our resting pulse rate drops significantly.

Regular exercise is also one of the best ways to counter the effects of aging, according to studies by the American Physical Therapy Association, Geriatrics Section. The person who exercises regularly is stimulating bone and muscle tissue and keeping them strong and flexible.

Exercise can serve many purposes. In choosing an exercise,

it is important to know what you hope to get out of it and whether that choice will help you achieve the desired outcome. The clearer you can be with what you want to achieve, will help to discover the optimum exercise program that is right for you. Know that any kind of motion involves the expenditure of calories and the more you move, the more calories you burn. You don't have to sweat profusely to use energy. In fact, walking a mile burns the same number of calories as running a mile. Your choice of an exercise program will depend on the time you have available in any given day, your age, your health and present physical condition and of course your bodies capabilities.

There are many benefits of exercising. It enhances a sense of total well-being. It will improve your mental outlook, and you will feel better. Exercise burns extra calories, not only during the exercise itself but also throughout the day. It creates efficient heartbeats. It reduces stress levels.

Movement of large muscles through exercise reduces muscle tension, thereby improving relaxation while improving alertness to undertake challenges.

Exercise improves concentration; it stops worry; it eases the mind, slows worry, allows for a new perspective. It exchanges quality of life for chances of disease. Exercise reduces the risk of many diseases such as: some cancers, heart attack, stroke, high blood pressure, and diabetes.

I pray that all may go well with you, and that you may be in good health, just as it is well with your soul.

So, my friend, if you do not have a regular exercise regiment, I would suggest counting the cost of not having one.

Notes for Reflection & Application:

You Are What You Eat

"What? know ye not that your body
is the temple of the Holy Ghost
which is in you, which ye have of God,
and ye are not your own?"
1 Cor. 6:19

You Are What You Eat

As clergy, we are probably the most unhealthy eaters on the planet. We would do ourselves a favor if we were to cut down our consumption of at least four basic foods: sugar, salt, white flour and saturated fat.

Sugar is really empty calories. Sugar beets or sugar cane are healthy foods if we consume them directly. But when the sugar is refined or extracted from these plants, all the fiber and other nutritional substances are eliminated. All that the body gets after the refinement is empty calories that tend to throw our metabolism off balance. It is a proven fact that over consumption of sugar is the number one contributor to obesity and sugar diabetes strikes overweight people three times more frequently that those who maintain their recommended weight.

Salt is the next ingredient to avoid. It is hard to imagine junk food without salt.

Salt is the chief cause of some people's hypertension (high blood pressure). If it isn't stress elevating your blood pressure, you can believe it's salt. One of every two people in North America is sodium sensitive, meaning that their blood pressure is especially sensitive to salt intake. As an African American, male, I know first hand that high blood pressure affects us more than it does our Caucasian brothers. Studies have shown that one out of every three African Americans over eighteen has high blood pressure.

White Flour is that white powdery stuff that shows up in most of our baked goods (sorry, Dunkin Donuts and Krispy Kreme). It is considered a key contributor to diseases of the digestive tract. Approximately 60,000 people in the United States die of colon cancer each year. Deaths from this disease could be greatly diminished if we would consume far more fiber-rich foods than white flour. Just think for a moment how we make dumplings;

mix some white flour with water and you have a pasty substance that works like any glue. Eating products made with white flour is like eating glue. When we digest large amounts of white flour, our digestive tract has difficulty processing it through our system. It gets stuck in our system and begins to take up residence and decay. Don't be fooled by the term "enriched flour." It is another way of saying white flour that has been sprayed with several vitamins your body probably doesn't need. I thought I would never say this, but it's the bran and the wheat germ that your body needs! Even the label "Whole Wheat Bread" is deceptive. Bakeries can call bread whole wheat, if the third ingredient is whole wheat. Read the label: 95% of the bread in your average grocery store has as its first ingredient, "enriched flour." The next ingredient is water, by volume, you are getting very little whole wheat. Beware of noodles, pastas, cakes, cookies, and pies which most are made from enriched white flour too. If we were to eliminate the sugar, the salt, and the white flour from our diets, we would greatly increase our eating habits. Just think for a moment how a doughnut is made.

Take away the sugar, the salt, the white flour and the saturated fat, and all that is left is the doughnut hole (munchkins)! Try substituting fruit for those doughnuts each morning and watch the difference in your energy levels.

Restricting Fat Intake. Simply cutting down on the consumption of red meat helps a lot in lowering the fat in our diets. Countries where red meat is rarely consumed have one fourth the incidence of heart disease of countries where beef and lamb are eaten regularly. Rather than having red meat once a day, try limiting it to once or twice a week. Try using skinless chicken and fish as substitutions. If you have heart disease in your family, as I do, it is encouraging to know that there are some specific things to do aid in breaking that generational curse!

Good Nutrition helps maintain and build structural integrity and wholeness within the body. Nutrition is consuming the 45 essential nutrients, digesting and absorbing these nutrients, transporting the nutrients to the cell, metabolizing these nutrients and eliminating the waste, while maintaining proper weight. The human body requires more than 100,000 chemicals to perform all the different functions necessary to sustain a strong and healthy lifestyle.

Carbohydrates: There function is to provide energy, energy storage (short and long term), vitamin and mineral source. Sources: Fruits, vegetables, whole-grain products, pasta, legumes. Need: Carbohydrates should supply 55-65 percent of your calories. This is your bodies best source of energy.

Dietary Fats (lipids) This fuel source provides and carries essential nutrients (Vitamin A, D, E, K and linolic acid), provides for certain body structure, protects and insulates, and provides food repletion. Sources: dairy products, meats, poultry, eggs, oils, nuts, seeds and many snack foods such as potato and corn chips.

Protein. Proteins provide structure and regulates body process through enzymes and hormones. Animal sources include: meat, fish, poultry, eggs, and milk. Plant sources include: green vegetables and legumes. Protein should supply 12-15 percent of your caloric intake-about 3 ounces of beef or chicken per day.

Vitamins. Fat soluble (A, D, E, K) and water-soluble (the B vitamins and C) vitamins are organic compounds necessary for metabolic reactions within your body. While vitamins provide no actual energy, they facilitate the energy-releasing reactions that promote your body's growth, development, and maintenance.

Minerals. Your body needs 19 essential minerals. These are generally supplied through a balanced diet consisting of a mix if animal and vegetable products.

Major minerals, requiring more than 100 mg. A day are calcium, phosphorous, magnesium, sodium, chloride, potassium, and sulfur. Trace minerals have a daily nutritional need of less than 100 mg. These are iron, zinc, selenium, iodine, copper, fluoride, molybdenum, chromium, and manganese.

<u>Water.</u> Water is absolutely necessary for the efficient completion of every chemical; process in the body. Water is a source of minerals, a solvent and transporter of nutrients, a lubricant, a temperature regulator, a growth promoter, a catalyst, and an acid-base balance. You need at least 64 ounces of water every day. Caffeine-laden liquids do not count and even have an opposite effect as water.

Rev. Andrew L. Foster, III.
So, You've Answered the Call??

About the Author

Rev. Andrew L. Foster, III.
So, You've Answered the Call??

About the Author

The Reverend Andrew L. Foster, III., M.Div.

Rev. Foster's mission in life is to worship, honor and praise His Lord and Savior, Jesus Christ with his whole being! He wants nothing less than to give his all to Him; spending time with Him alone in prayer and in personal devotion reading His Word. God has blessed him with the most precious gift, his wife, and First Lady, Mrs. Lorraine V. Foster. His personal mission as a husband is to honor and protect her and love her as Christ loves the church. Being a godly father is the most important stewardship with which he has been entrusted. Rev. Foster strives to be the man and the father God has ordained, by living a life that is worthy of emulation for his children. Personal holiness and spiritual integrity are non-negotiables in his life. His on-going mission in life is to be the loving, servant leader God has called him to be.

Rev. Andrew L. Foster, III.
So, You've Answered the Call??

Rev. Andrew L. Foster, III is a native of Philadelphia, receiving his early education in the South Jersey School System. He is the 6th generation of Methodist pastors. He served in the United States Air Force for over 7 years as an Administrative/Management Specialist. He is a graduate of Peirce College in Philadelphia, receiving an Associate in Science Degree in Business Management, a graduate of Rutgers University in Camden, receiving a dual Bachelor of Arts degree in Political and Computer Science, and is a graduate of Eastern Baptist Theological Seminary in Wynnewood, PA, receiving a Masters in Divinity. Rev. Foster continues to avail himself to any and all continuing education workshops and seminars that will further strengthen his commitment to "study to show thyself approved."

Rev. Foster was the first African American pastor to serve at Clearview United Methodist Church (a multi-cultural appointment), located in the Eastwick section of Philadelphia.

Rev. Andrew L. Foster, III.
So, You've Answered the Call??

Guided by the Holy Spirit, Rev. Foster facilitated the non-existent Adult Bible Study and Sunday School ministries. He also served as the Assistant Pastor at Tindley Temple United Methodist Church, alongside, his spiritual father, Rev. Dr. Alfred S. Maloney, now a district superintendent in the East District of the Eastern Pennsylvania Annual Conference of the United Methodist Church.

Rev. Foster was very active in the youth ministry, visitation of sick and shut in members, assisting and leading Bible Study, preaching/teaching and creating relationships in the community. Rev. Foster, has served as the Associate Pastor of Janes Memorial U.M. Church in the Germantown section of Philadelphia, PA. He is currently Senior Pastor of Grace Community UMC in the city of Chester, PA.

Rev. Foster is blessed to be married to his best friend and partner in ministry, Lorraine Foster.

They have three sons, Nathaniel, Andrew IV., and Joshua, one daughter, Loretta, and one granddaughter, Angel and one grandson, Andrew V. Rev. Foster believes in the beginning God created relationships. He is a family man and a people person. Rev. Foster is blessed to have a gift of listening and spiritual discernment.

Rev. Foster finds encouragement knowing that the Lord has called him to preach the good news to all people in all places. (Luke 4:18,19) Rev. Foster's favorite scripture verses are: Proverbs 3:5,6 "Trust in the Lord with all your heart, and do not lean on your own understanding; in all thy ways acknowledge Him, and He will direct your paths," and Proverbs 3:27 " Do not withhold good from them that deserve it when it is in your power to render aid."

Rev. Foster starts off his day with a prayer that helps to keep him focused and humbled in ministry:

Rev. Andrew L. Foster, III.
So, You've Answered the Call??

"Good Morning Lord; this is <u>Your</u> day. I am <u>Your</u> child, show me <u>Your</u> way. What's on the agenda for today? Can I be a part of it? To be of service to <u>You</u> and <u>Your</u> people."

His hobbies are reading, computers, electronic gadgets, music, roller skating, bowling, good Christian conversation and spending quality and quantity time with his family.

Suggested Books to Read

"Wisdom is the principal thing; therefore get
wisdom: and with all thy getting get
understanding."

Proverbs 4:7

Rev. Andrew L. Foster, III.
So, You've Answered the Call??

Suggested Books to Read

The Holy Bible – your favorite translation.

Benson, Herbert and Eileen M. Stuart. The Wellness Book: A Comprehensive Guide to Maintaining Health and Treating Stress-Related Illnesses. New York: Simon and Schuster Trade, 1993.

Colbert, Don. What Would Jesus Eat? Nashville, TN: Thomas Nelson, Inc., 2002.

Harbaugh, Gary L., Pastor As Person: Maintaining Personal Integrity in the Choices and Challenges of Ministry. Minneapolis, Augsburg Publishing House

Hands, Donald R., and Wayne L. Fehr. Spiritual Wholeness for Clergy: A New Psychology of Intimacy with God, Self and Others. Bethesda, MD: Alban Institute, Inc., 1993.

Rev. Andrew L. Foster, III.
So, You've Answered the Call??

Jones, Kirk. Rest in the Storm: Self-Care Strategies for Clergy and Other Caregivers. Valley Forge: Judson Press, 2001.

Melander, Rochelle, and Harold Eppiley. The Spiritual Leader's Guide to Self-Care. Bethesda, MD: Alban Institute, Inc. 2002.

Oswald, Roy. Clergy Self-Care: Finding a Balance for Effective Ministry. Bethesda, MD: Alban Institute, Inc. 1986.

Paulsell, Stephanie. Honoring the Body: Meditations on a Christian Practice. San Francisco: Jossey-Bass, Inc., 2002.

Rediger, G. Lloyd. Fit to Be a Pastor: A Call to Physical, Mental, and Spiritual Fitness. Louisville, KY: Westminister John Knox Press, 2000.

Rev. Andrew L. Foster, III.
So, You've Answered the Call??

Notes for Reflection & Application:

Rev. Andrew L. Foster, III.
So, You've Answered the Call??

Notes for Reflection & Application:

Rev. Andrew L. Foster, III.
So, You've Answered the Call??

Notes for Reflection & Application:

Rev. Andrew L. Foster, III.
So, You've Answered the Call??

Notes for Reflection & Application:

Rev. Andrew L. Foster, III.
So, You've Answered the Call??

Notes for Reflection & Application:

ISBN 1412073618

9 781412 073615